Quiet
Moments
FOR YOUR SOUL

STEVE CHAPMAN
PHOTOGRAPHY BY JOHN MACMURRAY

HARVEST HOUSE™PUBLISHERS

EUGENE, OREGON

D E D I C A T I O N :

To Lindsey Williams, who skillfully captured the vision for *Hymns from God's Great Cathedral*.

QUIET MOMENTS FOR YOUR SOUL
Text copyright © 2004 by Steve Chapman
Published by Harvest House Publishers
Eugene, Oregon 97402
www.harvesthousepublishers.com

Library of Congress Cataloging-in-Publication Data

Chapman, Steve.
  Quiet moments for your soul / text by Steve Chapman.
     p. cm.
Includes bibliographical references.
  ISBN-13: 978-0-7369-0373-8
  ISBN-10: 0-7369-0373-9 (alk. paper)
  1. Consolation. 2. Christian life. 3. Chapman, Steve. I. Title.
  BV4905.3.C48 2004
  242--dc22

                    2003014759

All photography is copyrighted by John MacMurray and may not be reproduced without the photographer's permission.

Design and production by Terry Dugan Design, Minneapolis, Minnesota

Scripture quotations are taken from the New American Standard Bible ®, © 1960, 1962, 1963, 1968, 1971, 1972, 1973, 1975, 1977 by The Lockman Foundation. Used by permission (www.Lockman.org); from the New King James Version, copyright © 1982 by Thomas Nelson, Inc. Used by permission. All rights reserved; from the *Holy Bible*, New Living Translation, copyright © 1996. Used by permission of Tyndale House Publishers, Inc., Wheaton, Illinois 60189 USA. All rights reserved; and from the King James Version of the Bible.

Printed in China.

07 08 09 10 11 12 13 /IM/ 10 9 8 7 6 5 4

Contents

Comfort for a Troubled Heart 4

1. The Shore 6
   The Doxology

2. A Safe Place 10
   For the Beauty of the Earth

3. The Song of the Spring 14
   Come, Thou Fount of Every Blessing

4. Wind and Wings 18
   Be Still, My Soul

5. Stars 24
   When He Cometh

6. Sail with Me 28
   Abide with Me

7. The Sound of Grace 32
   Amazing Grace

8. The Highest Mount 36
   Sweet Hour of Prayer

9. Near the Fire 40
   Nearer, My God, to Thee

10. For All the Senses 44
    Fairest Lord Jesus

Comfort for a Troubled Heart

THE HEAVENS
ARE THINE, THE
EARTH ALSO IS
THINE; THE WORLD
AND ALL IT
CONTAINS, THOU
HAST FOUNDED
THEM.

—PSALM 89:11

Where can the brokenhearted go to find comfort? One very worthy answer is found by following the footsteps of Jesus, the Good Shepherd, to the place He went after He heard the sad news of His cousin's cruel fate. After John the Baptist was beheaded by Herod's sword, the Scriptures report "He [Jesus] withdrew from there, in a boat, to a lonely place by Himself…" (Matthew 14:13).

His intention was solitude…sought in the silent sanctuary of His Creation…to go there to mourn and for a while to be with His heavenly Father.

Though hindered at first by the pressing needs of the throngs that literally chased Him as He went, Jesus did not lose the desire, nor the determination, to eventually be alone.

After fulfilling His compassion for the multitudes by feeding them with the food of miracles, before sending them away, He again turned His face to the stillness. This time, "He went up to the mountain by Himself to pray; and when it was evening He was there alone" (Matthew 14:23).

There are times when grief comes to us all. When it does, our hearts are often drawn to man-made temples…places that are very commendable attempts to provide a beautiful representation of God's holy, trustworthy, and comforting presence. But Jesus, who was burdened by sorrow, leads His followers instead to a place that is a much more astounding picture of the presence of the Almighty. He went to God's Great Cathedral… where the skies are His stained glass, the meadows are His pews, the rivers His baptistery, the mountains His pulpit. And, the music…Oh, the sweet comforting music that comes from the voices of His Creation. It is music that can both rapture the heart and settle the spirit in the very same instant. Poet and friend Darrell Harris writes about a few of the skilled musicians in that orchestra…

Whippoorwill windsong
Trumpeter swan
Tympani rumble of thunder and hoof
A cricket chorus
The viola tone of breeze in the elms
The music of God's Great Cathedral[1]

Are you filled with sorrow as Jesus was? If so, there is a place for you to go to find solace. Step outside…take your broken heart to the openness of the temple God has made.

Even if the needs of others cause delay, meet them, and then go for a while into…God's Great Cathedral. It will remind you of the One who alone is able to comfort your troubled heart.

Steve Chapman

FOR SINCE THE CREATION OF THE WORLD HIS INVISIBLE ATTRIBUTES, HIS ETERNAL POWER AND DIVINE NATURE, HAVE BEEN CLEARLY SEEN BEING UNDERSTOOD THROUGH WHAT HAS BEEN MADE.

—ROMANS 1:20

THE DOXOLOGY

Praise God, from whom all blessings flow
Praise Him, all creatures here below
Praise Him above, ye heavenly hosts
Praise Father, Son, and Holy Ghost

C H A P T E R   O N E

The Shore

The ocean edge.
    The edge of land.
        The great shore.
            I had never been there.

As a young inlander from Appalachia who preferred the security of solid ground beneath me, I couldn't help but notice the soft, water-soaked sand that tried to swallow my bare feet when a wave washed in. The instability made me keenly aware that I had arrived at a place on the earth where that which is uncertain meets with that which is certain. Yet, I was comforted because the shore was in control. Try as they did to overcome the land, the roaring waters that approached had their limits...and I was not afraid.

I stood for a long while and simply watched and listened to the rolling waves as they came in. Their arrival was rhythmic...faithful...predictable...even threatening. And, their voices seemed able to sing every note of the sound spectrum. I could hear nothing else.

That day as I looked out across the waters, a single, distant wave caught

WHO ENCLOSED

THE SEA...

AND I SAID,

"THUS FAR YOU

SHALL COME,

BUT NO FARTHER;

AND HERE SHALL

YOUR PROUD

WAVES STOP..."

—JOB 38:8,11

MORE THAN THE
SOUNDS OF MANY
WATERS, THAN THE
MIGHTY BREAKERS
OF THE SEA,
THE LORD ON
HIGH IS MIGHTY.

—PSALM 93:4

my attention. It appeared, grew quickly, and broke toward me. I decided to follow that one wave all the way to the shore. I kept my eyes on it only…merely one among the innumerable that have approached those ancient banks. The foreboding swell finally arrived. And when it did, I saw that it was promptly consumed by the sand. In that moment I mentally wrote this verse…

> Of all the waves that reached the shore
> I noticed only this one
> And it, too, disappeared.

So does trouble. Though it forms…builds…and arrives in full force, it can be swallowed in the same way the shore devours a wave. And, amazingly, the shore does more than just break the power of the breaker. It also manages to retain the welcomed resources that are delivered amid the watery, tumbling chaos. Food for the seagulls and collectibles, such as colorful seashells, for the humans who joy in finding such treasures.

Like waves, trouble does come. Perhaps at this hour, you have focused your eyes on a particular swell that is approaching…maybe it is even very near. Of all the sorrows that have ever threatened mankind, you notice especially this one…because it is headed to the place where you stand.

Take comfort…God is like the shore. He is acquainted with trouble, and He will not be overtaken by it. He will consume that wave. He is its limitation. It, too, will disappear into His care. You will not sink.

Furthermore, He will take resources from the wave and will feed you with the joy of knowing He cares for you. And those who are near will

find in your life the valuable souvenir of a testimony to His triumph
over sorrow.

The sound of the ocean surf. From now on may it be a voice that
serves as a reminder that when trouble breaks toward you, if you are
found standing on the Shore, He will not let it win over you.
He controls the waves.

Praises be to Him alone because He has said…

"In this world you will have tribulation, but be of good cheer, for I
have overcome the world" (John 16:33).

FOR THE BEAUTY
OF THE EARTH

For the beauty of the earth

For the glory of the skies

For the love which from our birth

Over and around us lies

Lord of all, to Thee we raise

This our hymn of grateful praise

CHAPTER TWO

A Safe Place

Emotionally badgered, verbally beaten, and tortured with unkindness, our son walked through the front door of our house one autumn afternoon. He had spent the day in one of the most hostile environments known to young men...school...in the eighth grade.

His face revealed the stress he had endured, and his mother saw it. The hunger for comfort was obvious, and she fed that hunger...with cookies...motherly manna.

After our son's spirit had enjoyed the care and the calm for a while, he said, "Thanks, Mom. No matter what they do to me at school, I know when I come home, I'm safe."

Home is supposed to be just that...a safe place...where meanness is not permitted, no verbal shoving is allowed, and hungers of all sorts are satisfied...a place where a weary child can go to feel at peace once more.

God also has children who have been wounded and beat up by the world. Where can they go to find comfort? They can go home...to God's presence...the safest place in the universe.

IN THEE, O LORD, I HAVE TAKEN REFUGE...

—PSALM 31:1

FOR IN THE
DAY OF TROUBLE
HE WILL
CONCEAL ME IN
HIS TABERNACLE;
IN THE SECRET
PLACE OF HIS
TENT HE WILL
HIDE ME...

—PSALM 27:5

There the heavenly Father sees their hunger for consolation, and He feeds it...with manna...cookies, you might say...Fatherly comfort food...that is, the sweetness of His nearness.

Thankfully, there are earthly pictures of that safe place. They are found in the beautiful, created majesties that reflect the eternal power and divine nature of a loving and caring God. A mighty mountain, a green field of healthy wheat, a thirst-quenching brook, the light of a starry expanse, a grove of fruit-laden trees where birds sing with satisfaction. Glorious places like these have a way of reminding the created that the Creator still lives and is nearby...and to be near Him, where He is, is safety.

Where I live, as the work week comes to an end, especially in the fair-weather seasons, I see many souls who have been at battle with life running out to enjoy nature. I am often among those who retreat. There's a farm, for example, among the hills of Tennessee, where I love to go and enjoy the sights and sounds. On that farm is a mountaintop that provides an incredible view. The ascent to the summit seems endless to muscles not often enough challenged by the climb. But what awaits at the peak is worth the effort. So I press on, ignoring the burning in my calves, aware that with each step upward I grow closer to the spot where I will be embraced by the grandeur.

I arrive...alone at the top. The sun brilliant...the valley unbelievably wide...the soft breeze a gentle relief...and I rest...engulfed in the beauty. At the top of the world...but submerged in splendor. And the view reminds me to say to the Maker of it all, "Thank You, Father, for the beauty of this place. And, no matter what they do to me down there, I know that when I'm at home with You, I feel safe. So please go with me when I descend from this mountain. Help me to always dwell in Your presence."

Guard me, O my Father
Let me sleep in Your care
I will not rest
Unless I know You're there

And in the quiet hours
When I'm helpless to defend
Guard me, O my Father
Until I wake again[2]

COME, THOU FOUNT
OF EVERY BLESSING

Come, Thou Fount of every blessing
Tune my heart to sing Thy grace
Streams of mercy never ceasing
Call for songs of loudest praise
Teach me some melodious sonnet
Sung by flaming tongues above
Praise the mount, I'm fixed upon it
Mount of Thy redeeming love

The Song of the Spring

On a friend's farm, not too far from our home, is a spring that has been active year-round for centuries. In the wet seasons I have seen its waters gush out of the hillside with a deafening roar. The volume of flow that mysteriously makes its way to the rocky opening is an impressive sight to behold.

But more amazing than that is what the spring does in the most searing, dry heat of summer. It is then, when the farm's free-standing ponds have been absorbed by the scorching sun, that a cold, steady stream still bubbles out of the side of the hill.

There's a song in the fountain during the summer. It has a gentle, lilting lyric that seems to say, "I will take care of you." Day and night…season by season…the constant melody of provision is directed to the creatures of the land.

Whitetail deer, raccoons, squirrels, and even unwelcome coyotes come to the song…and I have been at the stream's edge when many of them have quietly approached it. I stay motionless as I watch them find rescue

FOR WITH THEE
IS THE FOUNTAIN
OF LIFE…

—PSALM 36:9

15

THEY DID NOT
THIRST WHEN HE
LED THEM
THROUGH THE
DESERTS. HE
MADE THE WATER
FLOW OUT OF
THE ROCK FOR
THEM...

—ISAIAH 48:21

from the danger of deadly thirst. Then, as carefully as they came, they return silently satisfied to their fields and trees.

The birds of many feather come too. But when the birds gather around the flow to drink and enjoy, they are not silent. They sing back, and they do so with abandon as they musically call out words that sound like "Thank you...thank you!"

I love being at that hillside fountain on an early summer morning when the birds add their grateful melodies to the song of the giving spring. What a chorus! And when I hear it, I am reminded that I, too, have cause to sing.

In the driest of times, such as grief...doubt...fear...lack, the fountain of God's boundless blessings remains faithful in its flow. It rescues my thirsty heart. His spring sings to me, "I will take care of you."

He alone is the source of the waters of mercy...they never cease. His ever flowing grace covers my sins...forever. And His love pours forth in abundance when I feel like a failure...how often I need it.

So...at His spring I add my voice to the choir of myriad others who are grateful...and we sing, "Thank You, thank You..."

Will you join in?

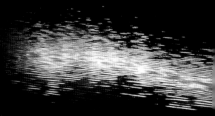

BE STILL, MY SOUL

Be still, my soul: the hour is hastening on
When we shall be forever with the Lord
When disappointment, grief, and fear are gone
Sorrow forgot, love's purest joys restored
Be still, my soul, when change and tears are past
All safe and blessed we shall meet at last

CHAPTER FOUR

Wind and Wings

Like a hungry wolf, death howled in the night. My loved one was being pursued. I tried to repel the beast with the torch of my prayers, but the bitter winds of sorrow extinguished the flames. Sadly, by the time morning came I had bid a reluctant farewell to my precious one. The day arrived dreary and cloudy. I cried…with the wind.

I wondered, as the volume of sadness grew in my soul, would the gale force of sorrow ever go away…would my heart ever feel the quiet calm again? I had my doubts…until the Lord of the winds appeared.

He came to me, not in bodily form, but in words. He who spoke to the rebellious sea winds, and they obeyed Him, this One found me in my distress and whispered a sonnet of hope to my soul.

> "Your loved one is not lost…only sleeping
>   inside My care…out of the wind,
>   far above the wolf.
>   Rest your heart. And
>   here is your hope," He whispered.

HOW PRECIOUS IS THY LOVINGKINDNESS, O GOD! AND THE CHILDREN OF MEN TAKE REFUGE IN THE SHADOW OF THY WINGS.

—PSALM 36:7

"While the angry wind
  brought suffering to you, I gave
  strength to the wings of your precious one
  to sail on that current of sorrow
  into My presence.
I prepared a place for them. I am here…
  they are here also. Let the cries of your
  soul subside…be still, My child…
  so you can listen for the wind.
And whenever you hear it, let it
  remind you of the flight your loved one has
  taken to the shelter of My wings."

The calm did finally return to my soul. I take great comfort in knowing that the one who is absent from me is present with the Lord. The thought of them waiting for me in Heaven did indeed bring stillness to my crying heart.

I believe I will see them again…when it comes my turn to take flight. Until then, I will be grateful for…wind and wings.

BE STILL, AND
KNOW THAT I AM
GOD.

—PSALM 46:10
NKJV

FOR THE LORD HIMSELF WILL DESCEND FROM HEAVEN WITH A SHOUT, WITH THE VOICE OF THE ARCHANGEL, AND WITH THE TRUMPET OF GOD; AND THE DEAD IN CHRIST SHALL RISE FIRST. THEN WE WHO ARE ALIVE AND REMAIN SHALL BE CAUGHT UP TOGETHER WITH THEM IN THE CLOUDS TO MEET THE LORD IN THE AIR, AND THUS WE SHALL ALWAYS BE WITH THE LORD.

—I THESSALONIANS 4:16-17

WE WILL FLY

Resting beneath the ground
Waiting to hear the sound
That the trumpet will make
Then they'll awake
And arise

Together we'll meet them in the air
And the Savior of us all will be there
Every sorrow we have known
In that moment will be gone
And we will fly

We will fly away
We will fly away
I'm longing for that day
When we fly away

And among those who rest in quiet sleep
Are the faces of ones so dear to me
There's comfort in this truth I know
The grave will let them go
And we will fly...

We will fly away
We will fly away
I'm longing for that day
When we fly away[3]

WHEN HE COMETH

When He cometh, when He cometh, to make up His jewels
All His jewels, precious jewels, His loved and His own
Like the stars of the morning, His bright crown adorning
They shall shine in their beauty, bright gems for His crown

Little children, little children, who love their Redeemer
Are the jewels, precious jewels, His loved and His own
Like the stars of the morning, His bright crown adorning
They shall shine in their beauty, bright gems for His crown

Stars

The darker the night, the brighter shine the stars. This is a truth that city dwellers can often forget. They live where things like streetlamps, headlights, and flashing neon signs all work together to absorb the view of the quasar set against a beautiful, black night sky. In order to see the true brilliance of the innumerable distant suns that sparkle in the evening heavens, they have to travel well outside the limits of their cities…a trip worth making.

My son and I were nearly 2000 miles from our Tennessee town one night. We were camped on a mountain in Montana…nowhere near anything glowing with artificial, man-made illumination. As we sipped some hot coffee outside our tent, we both, nearly at the same moment, looked up. Above us was an unbelievable sight. There must have been at least a thousand times a thousand pinpoints of light. Dancing, shimmering, brilliant white diamonds in the sky. They were more noticeable than we had ever remembered, because, of course, they were contrasted against a backdrop of the deepest darkness our eyes had ever seen. We marveled at the sight until our necks protested with pain. It was hard to stop gazing upward.

"THEY SHALL BE MINE," SAYS THE LORD OF HOSTS, "ON THE DAY THAT I MAKE THEM MY JEWELS."

—MALACHI 3:17

25

Do Not Fear
for I Have
redeemed you;
I have called
you by name;
You are Mine!

—ISAIAH 43:1

God's children are like stars...shining brightest in the darkest of times...more easily noticed when the world around them is in the deepest night. Against the black, hopeless backdrop of famine, for example, those who come with food shine brightest to the hungry. In the dismal, unlit abyss of war, those who relentlessly cover the battle in prayer are stars that brightly shine to the eyes of the soldier. When the birthing of a child turns dangerous for mother and infant, and the confident hands of the medically skilled do their miracles, these are stars that shine against the terrible darkness of impending sorrow. Countless more stars like these could be mentioned that illuminate the desolate, lightless skies of our world.

Someday, we are told, God will come to gather up these stars to make them His own. His children, who at a distance might look little to the world...small like the stars we see above our planet at night...He will gather. But great are these gems...fireballs of His goodness...bringing light to remind all who see them that darkness has its defeating foe.

Its no wonder that God would want them for His own...He joys in their existence...He made them, and He will reclaim them.

Then they that feared the LORD spoke often to one another: and the LORD hearkened, and heard it, and a book of remembrance was written before him for them that feared the LORD, and that thought upon his name.
Malachi 3:16

ABIDE WITH ME

Abide with me! Fast falls the eventide
The darkness deepens, Lord, with me abide
When other helpers fail, and comforts flee
Help of the helpless, O abide with me

Swift to its close, ebbs out life's little day
Earth's joys grow dim, its glories pass away
Change and decay in all around I see
O Thou who changest not, abide with me

It was not the first time the disciples had seen the Lord calm the troubled waters beneath their vessel. They had set sail once before with Him aboard. As He slept a storm arose. They woke Him up and He stilled the sea. Little did they know it would happen again. Only this time, they were out there without Him.

Just after the 5000 were miraculously fed with five loaves and two fishes, the Scriptures record this scene:

> Immediately He made His disciples get into the boat and go ahead of Him to the other side to Bethsaida, while He Himself was sending the multitude away. And after bidding them farewell, He departed to the mountain to pray. And when it was evening, the boat was in the midst of the sea, and He was alone on the land. And seeing them straining at the oars, for the wind was against them, at about the fourth watch of the night, He came to them, walking on the sea; and He intended to pass by them. But when they saw Him walking on the sea, they supposed that it was a ghost, and cried out; for they all saw Him and were frightened. But immediately He spoke with them

AND HE GOT

INTO THE BOAT

WITH THEM...

—MARK 6:51

29

and said to them, "Take courage; it is I, do not be afraid." And He got into the boat with them, and the wind stopped (Mark 6:45-51).

I can only imagine that after they witnessed the Lord's authority over the storms for the second time, the disciples would not want to ever pull up anchor again if He wasn't aboard. "Sail with us!" I can almost hear them say it. "Don't send us out there alone!"

Could we all not empathize with those desperate sailors? To negotiate our life-ships on seas that can change from calm to chaotic in a moment's time requires the comforting company of the One who rules the weather. None of us knows what a day holds. Our boats could leave the harbor of home to sail on emotionally glassy seas at morning and by evening we may find our souls helplessly rising and falling on the fierce swells of uncertainty.

Has evening come for you and being "tossed about" is precisely how you feel? If so, keep in mind that the Savior has been watching you from the shores of Heaven. Take comfort. At this moment He is coming your way. Don't be afraid of Him, nor should you be embarrassed that you've tried to defeat the winds by rowing to safety under your own strength. Instead, invite Him aboard your vessel. He awaits your willingness to let Him show you once again that He has authority over that which has troubled your waters. He longs to hear you say to Him…at this moment and always…"Sail with me."

He said, "My presence shall go with you, and I will give you rest"
(Exodus 33:14).

THEN HE [MOSES] SAID TO HIM, "IF THY PRESENCE DOES NOT GO WITH US, DO NOT LEAD US UP FROM HERE."

—EXODUS 33:14-15

AMAZING GRACE

Amazing grace! how sweet the sound
That saved a wretch like me
I once was lost, but now I'm found
Was blind, but now I see

'Twas grace that taught my heart to fear
And grace my fears relieved
How precious did that grace appear
The hour I first believed

Through many dangers toils and snares
I have already come
'Tis grace hath brought me safe thus far
And grace will lead me home

CHAPTER SEVEN

The Sound of Grace

Thunder…without the wrath of the storm…is the sound of grace!

It was on the narrow, winding Red River in middle Tennessee that the reality of this divine irony became clear to my daughter and me. The morning was sunny when we put our canoe in the water. As we shoved off into the current to enjoy a half-day float, we knew there would be no turning back. All was well through the first hour and a half. We talked, laughed, fished, and enjoyed the quiet, peaceful view. But around the hour of ten, things changed rapidly.

The skies began to fill with ominous black clouds. Then, suddenly, thunder began to roll through the river bed. It looked as though we were going to get caught unprepared in a cold, hard, drenching downpour. Adding to that threat was the fact that the area was known for the treachery of flash-flooding as well as severe lightning strikes. Our hearts raced as we paddled faster and faster and watched the conditions worsen by the minute.

THOU ART A GOD OF FORGIVENESS, GRACIOUS AND COMPASSIONATE, SLOW TO ANGER AND ABOUNDING IN LOVINGKINDNESS

—NEHEMIAH 9:17

THE THUNDER OF HIS POWER WHO CAN UNDERSTAND?

—EXODUS 33:14-15

But something curious took place that morning. The darkened skies roared with intimidation but never did let go of the rain. Strangely, the wind that usually accompanies an impending strong storm picked up only slightly. The cool breeze merely rustled the tops of the tall leafy trees on the banks of the stream.

It was odd, too, that, even though all the signs that warn of an oncoming storm were present, the birds continued to sing and the cicadas held their steady summer chorus. While the heavens roared and rattled the very seats of our canoe, the creatures on the Red seemed completely at ease...but we continued to worry.

Thankfully, that morning the fury of the storm never did come, only the thunder. It was as if we had heard the song of an awesome power...but sung with the lyric of mercy. To put it another way, we felt that we had encountered the booming gavel of the Almighty Judge, but because the tempest passed without harming us we felt pardoned... pitied...loved.

As we removed our canoe from the water around noon, and carried it up the bank to the truck, we both agreed that it was the mercy of God that we didn't get blown or swept away that day. We had heard the thunder...been made very aware of His power...but we were spared the doom. We had experienced the amazing sound of grace.

SWEET HOUR OF PRAYER

Sweet hour of prayer, sweet hour of pray

That calls me from a world of care

And bids me at my Father's throne

Make all my wants and wishes known

In seasons of distress and grief

My soul has often found relief

And oft escaped the tempter's snare

By thy return, sweet hour of prayer

The Highest Mount

City dwellers…of all who live among us these are perhaps the most deprived of the joy of time spent in the openness of God's Great Cathedral. But surely they are the most hungry for it. For that reason, they receive a special grace…a bit of good news that needs a divine explanation.

Some of them live in places where they can look beyond their jagged concrete skyline and see the grandeur of distant mountain peaks. A beautiful…but painful sight…for more than a few. Many of their tired, busy minds often imagine driving down a road that would lead them out of the urban sprawl to some desperately needed solitude. However, far too many days, and even weeks, go by without ever leaving town. The truth is, for many of them, the mental pilgrimage is frequently made, but too often their bodies just cannot follow. Duties in their metropolis have penned them in…flesh and soul…and their weary hearts grieve.

Those who especially love to journey to the quiet of the mountains and, as Jesus often did, to pray there, have spirits that ache with a special

> BUT AS FOR
> ME, MY PRAYER
> IS TO THEE,
> O LORD, AT AN
> ACCEPTABLE
> TIME…
>
> —PSALM 69:13

37

JESUS LEFT THE
UPSTAIRS ROOM
AND WENT AS
USUSAL TO THE
MOUNT OF
OLIVES...
HE WALKED AWAY,
ABOUT A STONE'S
THROW, AND
KNELT DOWN
AND PRAYED...

—LUKE 22:39-41

38

intensity to go "up from the city." They know the eternal value of eliminating the earthly distractions in order to help them sense a closeness to God. In the pages of the Scriptures, they have seen their Savior "go to the mount," and they want to do as He did. But try as they may to imitate Him, their success is rare.

The following verses flow from the pen of a city dweller...one of God's own. While grappling with an unfulfilled yearning to be alone with Him on one of the tall summits of Creation, he came to a unique insight. For others who embrace the same desire for spiritual solitude, these words might yield an important, timely, and comforting truth.

My heart
   A great city
      Two the same...
Both filled with crowd and noise
     No quiet street
     No peaceful lane
To share with You, my Lord

So tell me where
   If that place be
     Can we commune a while?
And this
    My Savior
   Said to me,
"You need not go a mile."

"A crowded street
   A meadow fair
     Where shall we meet again?

To Me, My child
   What matters most
   It is not where
But when!"

He said, "I know you
   If you could
     Ascend a mountain high
   You'd leave at once
   I know you would
You'd meet me
Near the skies..."

"...But don't forget, my child..."
"What'er sweet hour
   You call My name
     And pour out all your cares
You've scaled the mount
    That's highest *when*
   You come to Me
In prayer."[4]

What a precious thought for the one who feels confined inside a city's limits. Though it is good to do as often as possible, a body does not have to travel to a far distant peak on the planet in order for the spirit to enjoy the communion of God's presence. He, Himself, has chosen to dwell in us, and He alone is the most tranquil mountain to which His children can go.

Even while standing on the corner of a crowded street, while working in the chaos of an office complex, while busily tending to the cares of life that home requires...a soul can ascend to Him. And His Spirit may be calling you at this moment, saying…"Wherever you are, now is a good time for communing!"

LORD, THOU HAST BEEN OUR DWELLING PLACE IN ALL GENERATIONS. BEFORE THE MOUNTAINS WERE BORN, OR THOU DIDST GIVE BIRTH TO THE EARTH AND THE WORLD, EVEN FROM EVERLASTING TO EVERLASTING, THOU ART GOD.

—PSALM 90:1-2

NEARER, MY GOD, TO THEE

Though like the wanderer, the sun gone down
Darkness be over me, my rest a stone
Yet in my dreams I'd be nearer, my God, to Thee
Nearer, my God, to Thee, nearer to Thee

There let my way appear, steps up to Heav'n
All that Thou sendest me in mercy giv'n
Angels to beckon me, nearer, my God, to Thee
Nearer, my God, to Thee, nearer to Thee

CHAPTER NINE

Near the Fire

A hiker tells this story:

Lost…I'm not sure how I got so far away from the main trail. Nothing looked familiar in the wilderness…yet everything looked the same. I was alone!

Scared…I ran out of daylight. The sun fell too quickly behind the western mountain. My very spirit shook with fear as the strange night sounds successfully threatened my bravery and challenged my better judgment. I wanted to run, but I knew each step would be unsure. Unseen cliffs could easily claim me.

Cold…My flesh was hardening as the temperature plummeted. I needed to move to stay warm, but movement had to be limited to an unhurried, deliberate walk. With the growing, unfriendly fear inside me and the hostile coat of frigid air that covered my skin…all I could do was slowly stumble along the ground…and shiver. I had never felt so helpless, so vulnerable, so sure of trouble. Then…hope came…

Suddenly my spirit was lifted by something that floated downward off

> BUT AS FOR ME,
> THE NEARNESS
> OF GOD IS MY
> GOOD; I HAVE
> MADE GOD MY
> REFUGE…
>
> —PSALM 73:28

41

the mountain with the falling night thermals. It was…smoke! *It has to be a campfire,* I said to myself. *If it's the last thing I do tonight, I will get near it!*

So I climbed, keeping the odor of burning wood in my path. Even though there was no trail leading to the smoke, I headed straight up toward it. I wanted to be near the light of the fire…to let it chase away the intimidating darkness. I had to get close to it to let it melt away the head-to-toe layer of icy air that hung around my body. And, I wanted the nearness of the dancing flames to protect me against the hungry inhabitants of the mountain. In addition, I wondered, *Might there be a friendly soul there at the fire who will empathize with my need to come to the blaze?*

After a full hour of fighting through thorny underbrush and climbing over the fat trunks of huge fallen trees, I saw the glow of the fire ahead. With my voice raised, but shaking, I called out to the human who had built the fire. In response, I heard not just one voice, but three yell, "OVER HERE!" The chorus was a delightful sound.

The three hikers greeted me with obvious concern for my condition. They graciously offered me a place among them, poured hot coffee, and draped a sleeping bag over my shoulders. I was, to say the least, one happy camper to be near that fire.

This hiker's story contains an encouraging picture for all of us who feel that we are lost, alone, and facing the dangers that lurk in the darkness of life's wilderness. There is a Divine Fire who reaches out to us…The aroma of His nearness is in the night breezes, His eternal light calls us like a beacon, His healing and renewing warmth radiates out to meet us as we draw close to Him. And because evil will not go near to God, He is the Flame who protects us from harm. That is why the voice of the

Lord in James 4:8 is so precious to the pilgrim. "Draw near to Me and I will draw near to you."

In every moment of time, especially in every night, the love of God glows with guiding light, reaches to us with a warm hand, and is willing to repel the evil that would claim us. Are you lost? Does your heart detect the aroma of His flame as it comes to you on the winds of love? If so, draw near to that fire…and He will reach out to you.

DRAW NEAR TO
GOD AND HE
WILL DRAW NEAR
TO YOU.

—JAMES 4:8

FAIREST LORD JESUS

Fairest Lord Jesus, Ruler of all nature
O Thou of God and man the Son
Thee will I cherish, Thee will I honor
Thou, my soul's glory, joy, and crown

Fair are the meadows, fairer still the woodlands
Robed in the blooming garb of spring
Jesus is fairer, Jesus is purer
Who makes the woeful heart to sing

CHAPTER TEN

For All the Senses

Baby leaves,
robin eggs,
warmth...finally,
smell of fresh-cut grass,
strutting Tennessee turkeys,
bursts of color in the flower garden,
the lilting evening chorus of pond frogs
...some favorite signs that a long winter is over.

Enduring the winter is like waiting in a grave tomb...for me, at least. The longing for days that are friendly to the skin grows more intense as the cold months pass. The desire to spend some time outside, unbundled in extra pounds of clothing, makes wintry nights last forever. So I wait in anticipation of the first signs that the days are growing warmer. And I enjoy it when it all starts to happen.

Our territory is at its loveliest in the spring...we have something to entertain all the senses. There's nothing like the sight of the blooming redbud trees lining our roadways and wild, yellow buttercups turning

FOR BEHOLD,

THE WINTER IS

PAST...

—SONG OF
SOLOMON 2:11

45

brown, drab fields into dance floors for the heart. The scent of hyacinth and honeysuckle permeates the air. The contented song of the birds replaces the sound of winter's quiet death. The mild touch of nature's perfect temperature on the skin provides a needed thaw. And the unique taste of the skillfully hunted, freshly picked, deep-fried, morel mushroom can satisfy a winter's worth of longing.

The delights of springtime are indeed glorious to the flesh. But nothing compares to the joys that can touch the spirit in this season. It is at this time especially, when crops are commonly sown, that thankful hearts celebrate the remembrance of the Divine Seed that was planted over 2000 years ago. And that seed has a name…Jesus.

Like any other seed, heaven's holiest of Grain first had to die before He was placed in the ground. The day of His dying and burial was, without exception, the saddest of all days. But…the power of new life that was in the Seed could not be contained. The winter of death yielded to the warmth of God's love for mankind and suddenly, on the third day, the life in the Divine Seed burst forth. *Up from the grave He arose!* Life anew…to bloom forever in our hearts.

Because of Him our spirits can see redemption, take in the aroma of mercy, be touched by the warmth of His grace, hear the calming sound of the song of hope, and be satisfied forever by the sweet taste of His redeeming love.

He is truly the Essence of spring. He is something for all the senses!

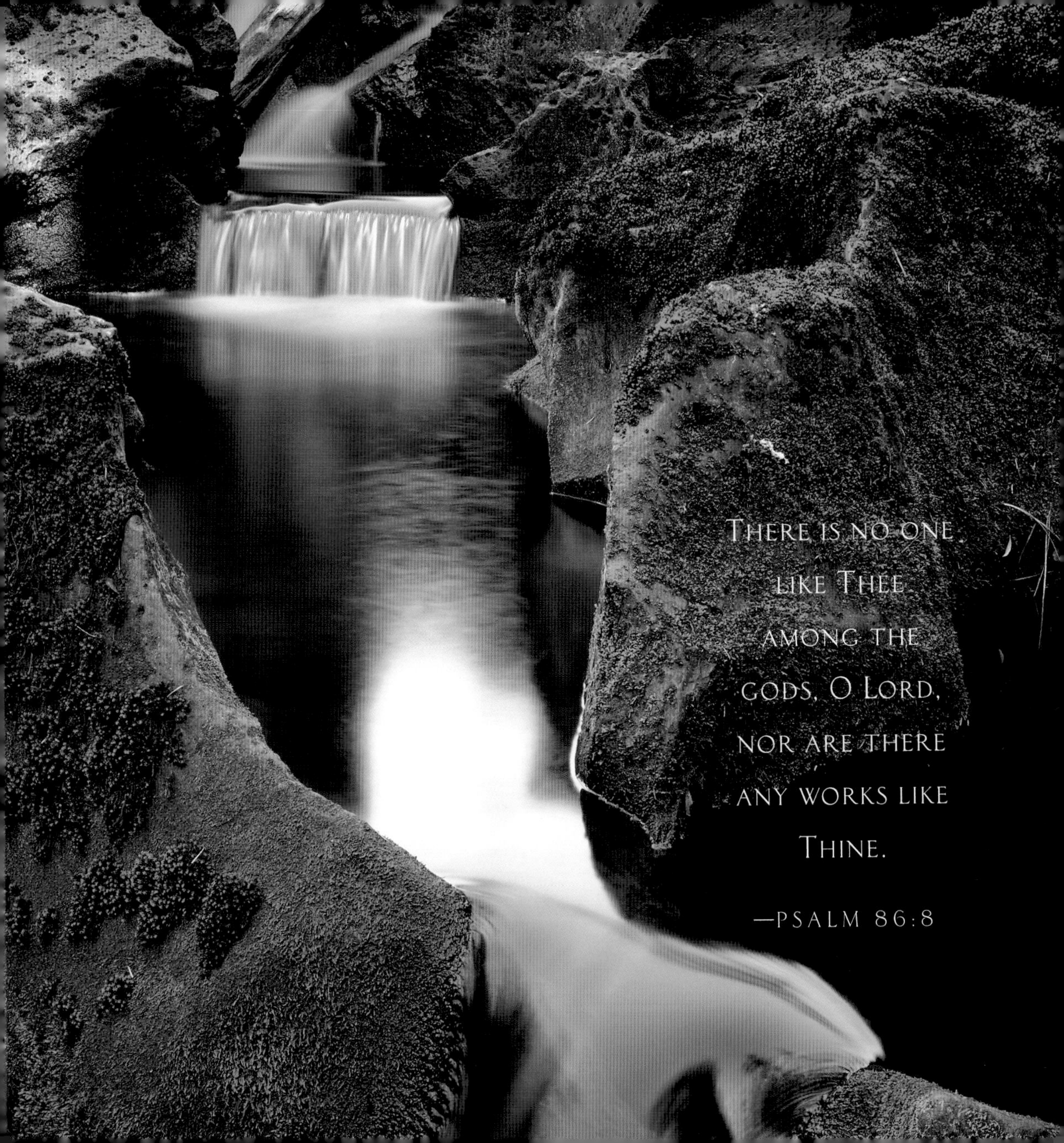

THERE IS NO ONE
LIKE THEE
AMONG THE
GODS, O LORD,
NOR ARE THERE
ANY WORKS LIKE
THINE.

—PSALM 86:8

Notes

1. "Whippoorwill Windsong," © 2003 by Darrell A. Harris.
All rights reserved. Used by permission.

2. "Guard Me," a poem by Steve Chapman/Times & Seasons Music/BMI 2003

3. "We Will Fly," words and music by Steve Chapman/Times & Seasons
Music/BMI 1996 (from the CD *Waiting to Hear* SACD-30)

4. "The Highest Mount," a poem by Steve Chapman/Times & Seasons
Music/2003